IF FO

👤 _____

✉ _____

📱 _____

Greater Than a Tourist Book Series
Reviews from Readers

I think the series is wonderful and beneficial for tourists to get information before visiting the city.

-Seckin Zumbul, Izmir Turkey

I am a world traveler who has read many trip guides but this one really made a difference for me. I would call it a heartfelt creation of a local guide expert instead of just a guide.

-Susy, Isla Holbox, Mexico

New to the area like me, this is a must have!

 -Joe, Bloomington, USA

This is a good series that gets down to it when looking for things to do at your destination without having to read a novel for just a few ideas.

-Rachel, Monterey, USA

Good information to have to plan my trip to this destination.

-Pennie Farrell, Mexico

Great ideas for a port day.

-Mary Martin USA

Aptly titled, you won't just be a tourist after reading this book. You'll be greater than a tourist!

-Alan Warner, Grand Rapids, USA

Even though I only have three days to spend in San Miguel in an upcoming visit, I will use the author's suggestions to guide some of my time there. An easy read - with chapters named to guide me in directions I want to go.

-Robert Catapano, USA

Great insights from a local perspective! Useful information and a very good value!

-Sarah, USA

This series provides an in-depth experience through the eyes of a local. Reading these series will help you to travel the city in with confidence and it'll make your journey a unique one.

-Andrew Teoh, Ipoh, Malaysia

GREATER THAN A TOURIST-ECUADOR

50 Travel Tips from a Local

Elaine Cheung

Cover designed by: Ivana Stamenkovic
Cover Image: https://pixabay.com/en/ecuador-guyayaquil-historic-district-
917102/

CZYK Publishing Since 2011.

Greater Than a Tourist
Visit our website at www.GreaterThanaTourist.com

Lock Haven, PA
All rights reserved.
ISBN: 9781791537425

>TOURIST

50 TRAVEL TIPS FROM A LOCAL

BOOK DESCRIPTION

Are you excited about planning your next trip?

Do you want to try something new?

Would you like some guidance from a local?

If you answered yes to any of these questions, then this Greater Than a Tourist book is for you.

Greater Than a Tourist- Ecuador by Elaine Cheung offers the inside scoop on all things Ecuador. Most travel books tell you how to travel like a tourist. Although there is nothing wrong with that, as part of the Greater Than a Tourist series, this book will give you travel tips from someone who has lived at your next travel destination.

In these pages, you will discover advice that will help you throughout your stay. This book will not tell you exact addresses or store hours but instead will give you excitement and knowledge from a local that you may not find in other smaller print travel books.

Travel like a local. Slow down, stay in one place, and get to know the people and the culture. By the time you finish this book, you will be eager and prepared to travel to your next destination.

TABLE OF CONTENTS

DEDICATION

This book is dedicated to my family. Thank you for allowing me to see the world and letting me return every once in a while for some home-cooked food. I would also like to dedicate this book to all the Ecuadorians who have contributed to this book with all their antidotes and endless trivia of their beloved country. ¡Muchas gracias por todo!

ABOUT THE AUTHOR

Elaine is an English teacher who has called a small Andean town in Ecuador home for the past year. She has also been published in several print magazines telling her tales of travel and the daily lives of locals. When Elaine is not working, she loves reading and attempting to be the next contestant on the "Great British Bake-off".

HOW TO USE THIS BOOK

The Greater Than a Tourist book series was written by someone who has lived in an area for over three months. The goal of this book is to help travelers either dream or experience different locations by providing opinions from a local. The author has made suggestions based on their own experiences. Please do your own research before traveling to the area in case the suggested places are unavailable.

Travel Advisories: As a first step in planning any trip abroad, check the Travel Advisories for your intended destination.
https://travel.state.gov/content/travel/en/ traveladvisories/traveladvisories.html

FROM THE PUBLISHER

Traveling can be one of the most important parts of a person's life. The anticipation and memories that you have are some of the best. As a publisher of the Greater Than a Tourist book series, as well as the popular 50 Things to Know book series, we strive to help you learn about new places, spark your imagination, and inspire you. Wherever you are and whatever you do I wish you safe, fun, and inspiring travel.

Lisa Rusczyk Ed. D.
CZYK Publishing

OUR STORY

Traveling is a passion of the "Greater than a Tourist" series creator. Lisa studied abroad in college, and for their honeymoon Lisa and her husband toured Europe. During her travels to Malta, an older man tried to give her some advice based on his own experience living on the island since he was a young boy. She was not sure if she should talk to the stranger but was interested in his advice. When traveling to some places she was wary to talk to locals because she was afraid that they weren't being genuine. Through her travels, Lisa learned how much locals had to share with tourists. Lisa created the "Greater Than a Tourist" book series to help connect people with locals. A topic that locals are very passionate about sharing.

WELCOME TO
> TOURIST

INTRODUCTION

One's destination is never a place, but a new way of seeing things. – Henry Miller

Ecuador is a small nation located on the equator in the continent of South America. With a mix of beautiful coastlines, indigenous villages dotting the Andes Mountains, the Amazon Basin tucked in its corner, and the magical Galapagos Islands, Ecuador offers travelers a little something for everyone.

1. GREETINGS, MEETINGS, AND ETIQUETTE

In Ecuador, depending on the time of day, you would greet with Buenos dias ("Good morning" in Spanish) in the mornings. Buenos tardes becomes a gray area. The literal translation is "Good afternoon", but Ecuadorians begin using it at 12:00 pm. Buenos noches ("Good night" in Spanish) usually begins around 5:00 pm.

When you greet an Ecuadorian for the first time, a sturdy handshake and eye contact are used. Once you become familiar with each other, men embrace then pat each other on the back or for women, use your right side of your face to kiss the left cheek of your greeter. Another common greeting between friends is the fist bump.

When you arrange a time to meet with an Ecuadorian, remember that they open the laws of la hora ecuatoriana (Ecuadorian time), which means that they will usually be late of up to an hour but still within the social limits of politeness.

Pointing at people with your finger is regarded as impolite. Use your entire hand or your chin to indicate the person you are talking about. However, pointing at an object with your finger is acceptable.

2. CURRENCY TO CARRY

Oddly enough, Ecuador uses the US dollar as their main currency. If you are bringing cash, make sure to get small denominations up to $20. When going to small shops or taxis, breaking a $20 bill will be very difficult as shopkeepers and drivers hardly ever have change. Usually, only hotels are willing to accept $50 and $100 bills. All banks in Ecuador are not willing to break large bills for non-banking customers.

When withdrawing from the ATM, look for machines located inside buildings as they are safer. Banco Pichincha and Banco del Austro do not charge any ATM fees on their end. You can withdraw up to $300-500 per day depending on the bank.

Credit cards can be used in Ecuador at major supermarkets like Supermaxi and Aki as well as the majority of shops inside malls. Many smaller shops will accept a credit card payment but often tack on an 8-15% fee on top of the charge.

3. A POCKET-FULL OF CHANGE

Ecuador began using the US dollar as its official currency in 2000 after a financial crisis caused extensive inflation. Afraid of counterfeit US bills from neighboring countries, many Ecuadorians began favoring coins, which lead to a huge demand of $1 coins entering the nation. Also, to meet the demands of changing currencies, Ecuador began minting their own coins in the same size, color, composition, and value as US coins. They only mint 1¢, 5¢, 10¢, 25¢, and 50¢ coins. This has become a problem in the US as Ecuadorian-minted coins have been brought into the country and have started circulating with the US currency.

4. WHAT'S IN A NAME?

The official name of Ecuador is the República del Ecuador, or "The Republic of the Equator", the only country in the world to have a geological feature as part of the name. Ecuador takes pride that the equator runs through the country, and in 1936, they built a monument to commemorate the 200th anniversary of its discovery on the equator. This monument was named Mitrid de Mundo (Middle of the World) located in Ciudad de Mitrid de Mundo (Middle of the World City) with a thick yellow line painted on the ground to show where the equator is located. In 1979, a 30-meter tower topped with a massive globe was erected to replace the aging memorial. However, much later, scientists discovered with the help of GPS technology that the supposed equator line was off by 240 m north. Now, you can visit both the real equator at the Museo de Sitio Intiñan where you can do lots of amazing science experiments to show the effects of being at the equator or the fake one, which is still called Mitrid de Mundo and is a great place to take photos of a tower.

In Ecuador, the sun always rises at 6:00 am and sets 6:00 pm thanks to the equator.

5. CLOSER TO SPACE

Earth is not a perfect sphere. Because of the Earth's rotation, the world bulges slightly at the equator. With everything else being equal, you are closer to space at the equator and farther from the Earth's core. This bulge makes Volcán (volcano) Chimborazo located in Riobamba 1.5 times higher than Mount Everest. Since mountains are measured at sea level, Everest is still the tallest the equatorial bulge makes the sea higher also.

6. ECUADOR'S FOUR DISTINCT REGIONS

Ecuador can be divided into four different geographical locations: the Andes, the Amazon jungle, the Coastal region, and the Galapagos.

Many of Ecuador's main attractions are located high up in the Andes Mountains along the Pan-American Highway. This includes the country's capital, Quito, which is perched 2,850 m above sea level, and Cuenca, a historical city with at 2,560 m high. Take a few days to acclimatize to the altitude to prevent altitude sickness. Symptoms include

19

headaches, vomiting, tiredness, trouble sleeping, and dizziness. If you need medicine, go to any pharmacy as tell them you have soroche, or acute mountain sickness (AMS). They will probably give you acetazolamide (Diamox), but it takes two days for it to start working. You can make tea with mate de coca (coca leaf tea) as a quick fix. These leaves can be found in any mercado (market).

The Ecuadorian Amazon area is mainly tropical rainforest that sits 400 m (1,312 ft) above sea level. This particular region is best visited with a tour or a guide as language and safety can be issues. The rainforest is hot and humid all year round with temperatures hovering around 26-35°C (79-95°F). The dry season is from December to March and is usually cooler than the rainy season. The main cities in the Amazon Basin include Tena in Napo province for Yasuní National Park and Lago Agrio in Sucumbios province for the southern part of the jungle.

Ecuador's coastal region spans more than 2,000 km (1,242 mi) long and is comprised of mangrove forests, charming fishing villages, and spectacular coastlines. The area is usually hot and humid with

temperatures averaging 25-31°C (76-91°F).
December to May is the rainy season, which is
warmer and humid. Popular beach cities include
Montañita, Quiteños, and Guayaquileños in Manabí
province and the less-visited towns in Esmeraldas
province to the north.

The Galapagos Islands sit on the equator where the
warmer southern trade winds converge with the
colder northern Humboldt Current. During the
islands' dry season from June to December, the water
is cooler and a layer of high atmosphere mist coves
the skies. Temperatures range from 18-23°C (65-
75°F). From January to May, temperatures become
more tropical with daily rain and cloudy skies,
roughly 21-27°C (70-80°F). This warm season is
when more marine iguanas, flamingos, and blue-
footed boobies are more prevalent.

7. THE AVENUE OF THE VOLCANOES

For a stretch of 321 km (199 mi) starting south of
Quito, there is an area known as la Avenida de los
Volcanes or the Avenue of the Volcanoes, which

contains nine peaks of more than 2,700 m (8,858 ft) high. The tallest of these is Chimborazo at 6,268 m (20,564 ft) last erupted in the 6th century. Cotapaxi, with its perfectly symmetrical cone, is the second highest on the avenue at 5,897 m (19,347 ft). It has exploded 50 times in the past 300 years, which has created several valleys from mudflow. Sangay, at 5,300 m (17,388 ft), has only erupted three times, but it only came to life in 1934. After a long period of inactivity, Tungurahua near Baños began rumbling again in 2000 and erupted five times since. It stands at 5,023 m (16,479 ft) tall and is considered one of the most active volcanoes in the world.

8. THE FIRST UNESCO WORLD HERITAGE SITES

Ecuador boasts the first and second World Heritage Sites. In 1978, at the first UNESCO World Heritage meeting, a catalog of 32 sites was determined for their inaugural list. The Galapagos Islands were the first on the list, and the second was the Quito's Historic Center.

In 1535, the Galapagos Archipelago was discovered when the Bishop of Panama sailed off course from Peru to Panama. For three centuries, the islands were used by pirates as shelter and to restock on water and food in the form of the giant Galapagos tortoises. In 1832, Ecuador annexed the islands calling it the Archipelago of Ecuador. Located 973 km (605 mi) from the mainland, the Galapagos feel like a world away. The Galapagueños, or the locals, referring to people from the mainland as la continente (the continent).

Quito's el Centro Histórico (Historic Center) is a collection of roughly 40 churches, monasteries, convents, and museums linked together by cobblestone streets all dating back to the early colonial days. In the heart of old town is Plaza Grande (or Plaza de la Independencia). Originally laid out in 1534, this plaza is surrounded by the city's catedral metropolitana, the Palacio de Carondelet (the Government Palace), the Archbishop's Palace, and City Hall. Protests are the norm in this plaza as many see it as a place to gather and be heard. On Sundays, the streets surrounding the plaza are closed off to traffic, making it a great place to people-watch locals in their Sunday best blending in with very fascinated tourists. La Ronda is considered one of Quito's oldest streets with its picturesque architecture and vintage charm. It still maintains some 18th-century artisanal homes as it is the bohemian center of the capital.

9. WHICH DAY IS ECUADORIAN INDEPENDENCE DAY?

The Spanish ruled Ecuador for nearly 300 years. When King Ferdinand VII of Spain was removed from power by Napoleon Bonaparte of France and then the title of the King was given to his brother, Joseph, the Spanish in Quito began to plan their revolt. On 10 August 1809, Quito stormed into the palace and declared its independence, making the city the first in Latin America to break free. However, 24 days later, the French regained control of Quito, a short-lived milestone. The news reverberated throughout the Americas and eventually led to movements to separate from their European conquerors.

On 9 October 1820, Guayaquil broke free and gained its independence permanently, the first city to do so in Latin America. The rest of Ecuador won their independence after winning the Battle of Pichincha against the Spanish Royalist Forces under the guidance of Antonio José de Sucre on 24 May 1822.

Today, the official Independence Day in Ecuador is called "la Día del Primer Grito de Independencia de Quito" (The first cry for Quito's independence) and is celebrated on 10 August to commemorate Quito's initial attempts at freedom.

10. THE COUNTRY OF GRAN COLOMBIA

After Ecuador gained their independence from Spain in 1822, they joined Colombia, Venezuela, and Panama to form the nation of Gran Colombia. It became the most prestigious country in Latin America. John Quincy Adams, the Secretary of State at the time, called Gran Colombia one of the most powerful countries in the world. However, several European nations did not consider Gran Colombia to be a legitimate state because they opposed the independence of their former colonies. Furthermore, Columbia and several international powers failed to agree over the extension of the Columbian territory and its borders. By 1831, the state was dissolved due to political differences over the type of government.

Gran Colombia broke up into New Granada, which later became Colombia, Venezuela, and Ecuador. In 1903, Panama gained their independence from Columbia. All flags of the initial three countries now bear similarities in color based on the flag of Gran Colombia.

The Ecuadorian flag is made up of three colors: yellow for the fertility of the crops and land in the country, red for the blood that was shed by soldiers to gain its independence, and blue to symbolize the ocean and the sky. In the center of the flag is the Coat of Arms of Ecuador, which has a condor perched on the top and Chimborazo Volcano in the middle.

11. ECUADORIANS ARE MULTILINGUAL

The official language in Ecuador is Spanish. However, Castilian, a variation of Spanish spoken in northern and central Spain, Quechua, an Incan language, and Shuar, a language spoken in the Amazon region are all recognized by the government as official languages for intercultural relations. In total, the government has written into its Constitution the preservation of 14 indigenous languages. They encourage these people the right to promote the use of their language in order to preserve their identity and their way of life since many of these indigenous languages cannot be translated in Spanish. It helps preserve particular and unique viewpoints.

There are nine different varieties of Quechua that are spoken by roughly 2 million speakers in mainly Chimborazo and Imbabura provinces located in the Andes Mountains. An estimated 35,000 people speak Shuar, and the language has been linked to several political organizations in Ecuador.

12. ECUA-SLANG

If you want to sound like a local, then you need to learn "Ecua-slang". Expats living in Ecuador often use the prefix "Ecua-" to emphasize something characteristically Ecuadorian. If you have a moderate level of Spanish, when talking with an Ecuadorian, they may throw in some Quechua words for a touch of humor.

¿Mande? means "Come again?" It has a negative historical background as Spanish conquistadors when subjects addressed their rulers with this word as the root word mandar means to command. Today, this word is considered polite and used every day.

¡Chuta! means "Shoot!" You say this when you are frustrated. If you want to stress more your frustrations, let out some more u's. ¡Chuuuuuuuuta!

13. NAVIGATING LIKE THE LOCALS

The best way to travel like a local is to take the bus. However, trying to figure out the bus system in unfamiliar territory can be daunting. For Guayaquil, Cuenca, and Manta download the app Moovit for all your bus needs. For Quito, your best is to use Google Maps for bus information. Always have change with you on the bus unless you like a lot of coins in your wallet.

Cuenca is the only city so far to have switched over to a card-based payment system. The Movilízate card costs $1.75 and can only be bought at certain locations like the main bus station. You must top up the card before it can be used. Another alternative here is to ask a local to tap twice and give the cost of the ride to that person.

14. PLENTIFUL TAXIS

In every Ecuadorian city, you'll find plenty of taxis. They are yellow and easy to spot. In larger cities like Quito and Guayaquil, some destinations may have preset rates and are non-negotiable. Others use meters. Another alternative you have an Ecuadorian phone number or data is to download ride-sharing apps. Uber is relatively new to Ecuador but offers the best rates. Cabify and EasyTaxi are other apps that many locals use to get around. These apps are mainly used in Quito and Guayaquil. Another newcomer that caters to both big cities and smaller towns is KTaxi.

15. WHAT TIME IS THE NEXT BUS?

The best way to get around the country is by bus. However, trying to find bus schedules on the Internet is next to impossible. For popular routes like Quito-Baños or Guayaquil-Montiñita, it's a safe bet that there will be a bus leaving every 30 minutes. At the bus station, you'll hear a man yelling out destination. If it isn't the location you want, they will point you in the right direction. The frequency of buses at night drop significantly past 9:00 pm.

Buses do leave on time, give or take five minutes. At some bus stations like Quitumbe (Quito) and Guayaquil, passengers are required to pay a tariff to go to the platform, which you pay with the ticket. However, in other bus stations like in Cuenca, you must pay the fee separately, which can eat into your boarding time if the machine doesn't work.

For larger items, stow your bags in the bus carriage. Tell the ticket guy your final destination, and he'll put your luggage in the correct compartment. In the bus, it is advised not to put anything of value in the overhead compartment as it can easily be stolen if you fall asleep. If you want to keep your belongings, place them on your lap or next to you with the bag strap around your leg.

There is onboard entertainment while on the bus. However, you have no say as to the movie choice or the volume of the audio. Bring earplugs if you intend to sleep through the noise.

16. BATHROOMS ON BUSES MAY EXIST

In the bus, there will be plenty of snacks to buy as vendors hop on and off the bus whenever they stop to pick up a passenger on the road. Some different types of snacks sold on buses include freshly baked banana bread and cupcakes, papas fritas (potato chips) with ketchup and mayonnaise, and popsicles. There is a bathroom on the bus, but 9 out of 10 times, the bus driver or ticket taker will tell you the bathroom key is broken and the door cannot be opened. For a 6-hour journey, the bus may stop once and wait for five minutes for passengers to board for the bus, but most times, these stops are far and few between.

17. PUBLIC BATHROOMS

Bathrooms in Ecuador are marked as baños or SS HH (the abbreviation for servicios higiénicos). Damas or mujueres are for women and caballeros or hombres are for men.

When you use a public bathroom in Ecuador, if you're lucky, sometimes papel higiénicos (toilet paper) is provided but it is not always in the bathroom stall. Look for a toilet paper dispenser outside the stall. Otherwise, bring toilet paper with you. And make sure to throw toilet paper in the bin and not in the toilet. The sewer system in Ecuador is not built to handle paper waste.

18. LAYERS ARE YOUR FRIENDS

Considering the size of Ecuador, it's quite remarkable how many different types of climate you can experience. In cities located on the Pan-American Highway, expect your mornings to be cold, midday to be warm then topped off with afternoon rain. If you head to the Amazon region, bring plenty of mosquito repellent and loose clothing for the heat. On the coast, the weather is warm and the sun is intense. Also, don't forget sunscreen. The equatorial sun is very strong, especially at high altitudes.

19. FREE WALKING TOURS

Many major cities in Ecuador offer free walking tours albeit some ask kindly for a tip at the end. In Quito, sign up for the Free Walking Tour by Community Hostel for a tour of the historic center or see different neighborhoods form Quito Street Tours. In Cuenca, there's the Free Walking Tour (no tip asked) from the city's tourist information board or the Free Walking Tour Cuenca. In Guayaquil, look up Free Tour Guayaquil. If you find yourself in Loja, do a tour with Free Walks/Loja. All these tours operate daily, Monday to Saturday.

20. GUINEA PIG, ANYONE?

Cuy or guinea pig is a delicacy in Ecuador. Generally, these furry creatures are roasted whole and turned by hand. Cuy is usually found in the countryside and can cost anywhere from $10-25 for a whole guinea pig. It has a gamey flavor and takes a bit of work to eat as there are lots of bones to work through. Cuy is usually served with potatoes and corn.

21. CHOCOLATE IS GOLD IN ECUADOR

A recent archeological study has suggested that the cocoa bean may have originated in Ecuador's southern Amazonian region of Zamora Chinchipe some 5,000 years ago. Only 5% of the world's cacao beans are considered "gourmet quality". Ecuador grows 60% of these fine beans. Farmers in the northern province of Esmeraldas call their cacao beans "black gold". Chocolate aficionados note that Ecuadorian cacao has a very complex floral flavor because of the terrain which the beans are grown on and the country's equatorial location.

Pacari and Republica de Cacao are quite famous in Ecuador and are readily available in most supermarkets in the country. Republica de Cacao has numerous branches in Quito and one in Guayaquil to sample some of their products and buy some uniquely chocolate items such as cacao soap and chocolate-scented candles.

Kallari, Hoja Verde, and Minka are also excellent Ecuadorian-based chocolate makers worth trying.

22. COFFEE LOVE

From the spine of the Andes Mountains to the low-lying Amazon Basin, on the tropical coast and even to the far-flung Galapagos Islands, coffee is grown everywhere. Coffee was first introduced to Ecuador in 1860 to the coastal province of Manabí. At the moment, coffee production is more focused on a smaller scale to produce specialty beans.

Loja, Zaruma, and Intag are well-known coffee regions in the country. Many fincas or farms in these areas offer tours of their plantations.

The most traditional way to make coffee in Ecuador is with a chuspa or bag in Quechua. The chuspa is made of linen and looks like a sock. The chuspa filter is placed on a ring stand with the coffee grounds placed inside the sock. Hot water is poured into the sock and the coffee is dripped into the cup below. Ecuadorians have been making coffee this way since the 18th century.

23. QUESO!

Queso (cheese) is very popular in Ecuador. The most common type of cheese you can find in the country is queso fresco molido (fresh ground cheese). Sold in every mercado, it can go for $2-3 depending on the size. However, the texture of this cheese may be off-putting for some.

There are also excellent cheese makers in Ecuador. Salinerito, based in the small town of Salinas de Guaranda in Bolívar province makes amazing mozzarella and is sold in major supermarkets in Ecuador. If you ever find yourself in Salinas, you can also sample their basil and ají (chili) mozzarella. Floralp is a Swiss company based in Ibarra province that makes a huge assortment of cheese.

24. BANANAS FOR BANANAS

Ecuador is one of the biggest exporters of bananas in the world. In 2016, the country made $2.7 billion in revenue with this fruit accounting for 23.3% of all banana exports worldwide. With 300 different varieties of bananas grown in the country, it is no surprise that bananas can also be found in many facets of Ecuadorian cuisine. Oritos are sweet bananas that are short and fat. Plátanos or plantains are usually cooked before it is eaten because of its tough texture. In the Ecuadorian coastal region, patacones, or fried plantains are a popular dish. Chifles are fried green plantains that usually are accompanied with ceviche. Bolon de verde is a green plantain dumpling that is usually served for breakfast. It is filled with cheese, chorizo (pork sausage), or chicharrones (fried pork rinds). Biche de pescado is a fish soup made of sweet plantains and is most famous in Manabí province.

25. CANELAZO, ECUADOR'S NATIONAL ALCOHOLIC DRINK

Canelazo is a traditional spiced drink that originates from the highlands of Ecuador. This warm drink is served at night when the temperature drops significantly. The recipe includes boiling water with cinnamon and panela, whole cane sugar then mixing it with punta or aguaridiente, local sugar cane alcohol. A popular version of canelazo is naranjillazo, which includes naranjilla, a very tart and acidic fruit.

An excellent place to try canelazo is in Quito's Historic Center on a cobblestone street called La Ronda, one of the oldest streets in the city or in the Guapulo neighborhood at any bar with a balcony overlooking Mount Cotohurco. Canelazo is also sold by street vendors in November and December during holiday and street festivals. If you find yourself in Cuenca, canelazo is very popular during "El Paso de Niño Viajero", the biggest Christmas festival in the country.

26. JUMPING ON THE CHIVA BUS

A chiva translates out to goat, and way back when, a chiva bus was a vibrantly-colored vehicle used to transport up to 45 people to and from places. However, in Quito, chivas are the ultimate party bus. These colorfully painted and well-lit buses are small commuter buses that have been converted into a moving party complete with a DJ booth, a stripper dance pole, and copious amounts of canelazo, the only alcoholic drink allowed on the vehicle. Sometimes, a live band manages to squeeze into the bus. Chivas drive around the city, mainly in Plaza

Foch and the Historic Center on Saturdays, as you dance, drink, and be merry. Baños and Guayaquil have also started jumped on the bandwagon with their own versions of chivas.

27. EATING OUT

The most economical way to eat out in Ecuador is to have your main meal at lunch like the locals. Almuerzos (lunch sets) usually include sopa (soup), jugo (fruit juice), segundo (the main dish), and sometime postre (dessert) for $2.50-$3.50, depending on the location and meal offered. You will almost always see something that is seco de (stewed) or fritada (fried) on any almuerzo menu. The selection of entrees includes pollo (chicken), carne (beef), costilla (ribs), and pescado (fish).

Vegetarians will find it difficult to find options but llapingachos (stuffed potato patties with cheese) is a safe choice. Chifas (Chinese restaurants catering to Ecuadorian tastes) also have a variety of vegetarian dishes to pick from.

Before you begin your meal with friends, say buen provecho (enjoy your meal) to everyone at the table. When passing someone in line, use con promiso (with permission).

In eateries throughout Ecuador, when you ask for the check, you are essentially telling the owners that their food was bad and you want to go. To not offend anyone, walk to the counter and tell the waiter what you had and pay there.

28. USUAL EATS OF ECUADOR

Many Ecuadorians consider guatita (little belly) as their go-to hangover cure after hitting the canelazo hard the night before. Guatita is a warm stew made of cow stomach with hints of cilantro, clove, sautéed onions, garlic, cumin, refrito (achiote power), and pasta de mani (peanut sauce). The dish is usually served with potatoes, rice, encuritido (salty pickled onions), and avocado. This dish is only served on Saturday or Sunday mornings.

Caldo de 31 (31 broth or caldo de manguera or de la vida, broth of the hose or life) is a soup that takes a day to make. A beef carcass including most of its organs is cleaned then simmered overnight in a clay pot with lemon to make the meat tender. People wait in line to get a bowl until it is sold out, which is usually by midday because so few establishments make this indigenous dish. The soup is served with well-cooked mote (a corn grain), potatoes, chopped herbs, avocado slices, and a slice of lemon. The broth is called caldo de 31 because at the end of the month, roughly every 31 days, hacienda owners cook one cattle they worked hard to raise. This ancestral dish is believed to help pregnant women or those who feel weak because the broth will help lift their spirits. This soup can be found in Otavalo or Ambato.

Fanesca is a soup served only during the Easter season in the Andes region of the country. This time-consuming dish is made out of salted cod that is cooked in milk then thickened with ground pumpkin seeds or peanuts. Then a dozen different beans, vegetables, or grains are added, each ingredient representing the 12 apostles. Each fanesca maker has their own blend of vegetables and legumes that is always top secret. The soup is served with hard-boiled eggs, pieces of plantain, and miniature empanadas. There are several stories linked to fanesca. One legend states that during the times of the ancient Romans, some Christians were caught sneaking into the catacombs with bags of grain and legumes to cook a soup in one massive pot. Another fable states that in the pre-Columbian Andes, people celebrated their harvest by putting as much as they could into one soup.

29. PANAMA HATS ARE NOT FROM PANAMA

In the mid-1600s, toquilla straw hat weaving began along the coast of Ecuador and in small towns throughout the Andes. Generally, these hats that were produced used toquilla palm or jipijapa palm leaves. In 1835, Manual Alfaro went to Montecristi in Manabí province to set up a hat export business. He filled cargo ships in Guayaquil and Manta with his goods and set sail to the Gulf of Panama. His business prospered as Gold Rush prospectors passing through Panama were looking for ways to protect themselves from the sun. Thus, they have named Panama hats because that's where they were sold and not the country of origin.

You can pick up your own Panama hat easily in Cuenca. There is the Homero Ortega Panama Hat Factory where you can tour the premises to see how these hats are made before ending at the factory store. Prices start at $40. There is also the Museo del Sombrero de Paja Toquilla, a small museum that explains the history of the Panama hat. There's also a store with a plethora of hats to pick from. If you're not hat-ted out, do a day trip to the Chordeleg Canton, which is about two hours away from Cuenca. This small village is one of the originators of the Panama hat and still continues this tradition today. Prices are cheaper also.

30. SHRUNKEN HEADS

Deep in the Ecuadorian Amazon lives a headhunting tribe called Jivaro. What makes this clan unique is they are the only group in the world to practice the ancient art of shrinking human and animal heads. They believe that shrinking the head of an enemy harnesses their spirit, which prevents the soul from retaliating and makes the enemy the slave of the shrinker.

The Jivaro tribe now limits their practice of shrunken heads to animals. However, if you want to see some shrunken human heads, head to the Museo de Sitio Intiñan in Quito or Museo de Pumapunga in Cuenca.

31. CLEANING YOUR AURA

Curanderos or faith healers are common fixtures in the Ecuadorian community. They use traditional indigenous medical practices with Catholic rituals. Many believe that curanderos have supernatural powers and illnesses are caused by lost spirits or curses. Since modern medicine and doctors are inaccessible to many Ecuadorians, curanderos often are the de facto health clinic.

There are several types of curanderos. Yerberos, the most common ones found in Ecuador, are mainly herbalists. Hueseros are bone and muscle specialists who focus on physical ailments. Parteras are midwives who help with childbirth.

A typical session with a curandero begins with a bouquet of herbs. For 2-3 minutes, the curandero beats you all over your body with the bouquet as they chant. For the second stage of the diagnosis, the curandero will ask you to expose your stomach and back so they can spit liquid at these two areas. Next, the curandero washes you with an uncracked egg. Since the egg is porous, it can absorb any negative energy from your body. They rub the egg all over your body. Afterward, the curandero massages you with a concoction of herbs and chili peppers soaked in alcohol. This is supposed to relax you to help finish the cleansing. The curandero gives you a diagnosis by cracking the egg into a plastic bag mixed with water in order to read the egg.

If you want to experience a session with a curandero, in Cuenca, go to the Mercado de las Artesanías Rotary. They are there every Tuesday and Friday starting at 10:00.

Back in 2008, Ecuador rewrote its Constitution recognizing the Rights of Nature, making it the first country in the world to do so. Rather than treating nature as a property of the nation under the law, the Rights for Nature acknowledges that nature in all its forms has the "right to exist, persist, maintain, and regenerate its vital cycles, structure, functions, and its processes in evolution." The people have the legal power to impose these inalienable rights on behalf of the ecosystems, which can be named as the defendant. Since this inclusion, other countries have followed suit including Bolivia, Turkey, Nepal, some parts of the US, and New Zealand.

32. GALAPAGOS ISLAND LIFE

Ecuador has taken great strides to preserve the Galapagos Islands as much as possible. Before you board your plane to the islands, please be aware that no seeds or dirt of any sort can be brought. This includes fruit, which contains seeds, and your hiking shoes should be thoroughly cleaned before it is packed. At the airport, all bags will be x-rayed and locked for the sole purpose to prevent organic matter that could harm the Archipelago. When you arrive in Baltra (airport code GPS) or San Cristabol (airport code SCY) airports, your bags will again be checked by trained dogs looking for anything that can hurt the ecosystem.

On the islands, there are attempts to recycle compared to the mainland. You will usually find three bins: green for organic waste, blue for recyclable items, and black for non-recyclable things. Articles in both the blue and black bins are flown back to the mainland for disposable.

Plastic bags are also hard to come by compared to the mainland. Proinsular Market, the only proper supermarket on Santa Cruz Island located next to the pier, does not supply any plastic bags. Most tiendas or stores will not give you one unless you ask. If you want to do some shopping at the mercado, bring your own bag.

33. WHO WANTS TO PLAY ECUAVOLLEY?

Ecuavolley is one of the country's beloved pastimes. As the name suggests, it is a form of volleyball invented by Ecuadorians. Its origins are uncertain, but many believe the sport began in the mountain regions. Since 1943, the sport is played in neighborhoods, parks, and streets all over the country. The sport is considered to be for the lower-class and particularly with taxi drivers and played almost exclusively by men.

Ecuavolley is played with a soccer ball. There are three people in each team: the setter, the server, and the flyer. The dimensions of the Ecuavolley court are the same as volleyball. The server can only serve with one hand and must shout "¡Bola!" right before the ball is served. The ball can only be held for one second, and the team has three chances to get it over the net. A point is awarded when the ball hits the ground of the opposing that served. The game lasts two sets with 15 points required to win the set.

To experience this sport, go to any park, especially in the evenings, sit down, and watch men fight tooth and nail for points. Everyone is welcomed to participate. However, the games can get intense, and depending on where they are playing a lot of gambling takes place. There are numerous tournaments and a national championship.

34. ECUADORIANS LOVE SWINGS

There is a child in all of us and what better way to feed our inter-child is on a swing. The most famous swing is at Casa del Arbol (Treehouse) in Baños. There is a bus at Calle Pastaza and Vincente Rocafuerte for $1 and enjoy the hour ride up. The entrance to enter Casa del Arbol is $1, but you will have four different swings to swing with Mount Tungurahua as your backdrop. The swing is safe and you can swing as long as your heart is content, or when the line starts growing. There is also a rudimentary zip line made of old rubber times that is good fun.

If you are looking for amazing views of Cuenca on a swing, there is El Columpio (the swing) located next to Mirador de Turi in Aventuri Park. For $1 to enter the park and $2 to swing, you get strapped into a chair with a seatbelt that is attached to two trees. Minus the questionable safety, you will get a panoramic view of Cuenca. There are also zip lines in the park, but the swing is the most memorable.

35. TRAINS

Trains are not commonly used in Ecuador. In 2008, only 10% of all trains in the country were operational due to flooding. Since then, the government has spent roughly $280 million to repair the railroads. These days, Tren Ecuador, the national rail company, caters its locomotives to tourists wanting to see spectacular views of the country.

Tren Crucero is a luxury train service from Quito to Guayaquil. This four-day journey takes passengers through the "Avenue of the Volcanoes" with views of Cotopaxi and Chimborazo before going through La Nariz del Diablo (The Devil's Nose), considered one of the most difficult train tracks to build. The trip continues onto the Ecuadorian coastline before finishing in Guayaquil. This journey costs $1,735 per person, but it includes food and accommodation.

For those looking for a cheaper way to experience Ecuadorian trains, it is possible to board sections of the Tren Crucero journey. The most popular trip is to go to the town of Alausí in Chimborazo province and board the train for La Nariz del Diablo. For $33, you can ride the train that zigzags around mountains with perpendicular walls and climbs 500 m (1,640 ft) in less than 12.5 km (7.76 mi) including steep ascents and descents before arriving in the small village of Sibambe. Then, the journey reverses taking you back to Alausí. This train twice a day and operates every day except Mondays. Another alternative to see La Nariz del Diablo train in action without the cost is to hike. The well-laid-out trail is easy; just start early as it is about 4 hours to get from Alausí to Sibambe.

36. THERMAL SPAS

Thanks to several active volcanoes in the country, Ecuador has a plethora of thermal hot springs to relax in. If you are in Quito, have a nice day trip in Papallacta, a small town located an hour away from the city. Located 3,250 m (10,662 ft) in the Andes, it is home to Termas de Papallacta, a spa resort which uses water from Chacana, a 3 million-year-old volcanic complex. The entrance fee for this spa is $23 per person.

Baños de Agua Santa commonly referred to as Baños, is located on the northern foothills of the Tungurahua volcano situated 5,023 m (16,479 ft) above sea level. This popular weekend getaway for Ecuadorians is home to more than 60 waterfalls and a plethora of thermal baths. Termas de La Virgin is a community project built in 1928. For the bargain price of $3, you can soak in several pools of various temperatures with a view of La Cascada de La Virgin in the background. However, these pools are only open early in the morning starting at 5-9 am and 6-9:30 pm. There is another Termas de La Virgin that is open all day and cost $6 per person. Every person who enters these baths must use a swimming cap, which costs 50¢ at any vendor across the baths.

Near Cuenca, there is a town called Baños de Cuenca (aka the other Baños) offers plenty of thermal baths for every price point. El Riñon Balneario offers their thermal baths for $5. A swimming cap is obligatory. Piedra de Agua offers a spa circuit of five different experiences. First, you sit in a sauna where temperatures reach 40°C (104°F). Then you are whisked away to a red mud pool where you slather yourself with warm red mud. Afterward, there is the blue mud pool where you do the exactly the same. After all that work, you soak in the underground contrast pools of lukewarm water and frigid cold water. The final step in the spa circuit is sitting in a steam box. This circuit costs $35, but if you go at 6-8 am every day or at selected times in the evenings on Mondays, Wednesdays, and Fridays with a friend, you can two for the price of one.

37. THE ECUADORIAN LAS VEGAS

The Las Vegas culture that lived about 10,000 years ago on the Santa Elena peninsula in Santa Elena province along the coastlines of the Pacific is considered one of the oldest civilizations in South America. This tribe comprised of hunters and gathers that developed basic agriculture, the first known group to do so. Archeologists believe they grew a semi-domesticated version of squash and maize. Their most prominent settlement was near the Rio Las Vegas.

To see the burial site of two people of the Las Vegas culture, visit Museo Amantes de Sumpa in Santa Elena near the city of Salinas. The museum also exhibits traditional arts and crafts around the coastal region of Ecuador. Entrance is free.

38. THE PYRAMIDS OF ECUADOR

The site of the ancient pyramids of Cochasqui is considered one of the most important archaeological sites in Ecuador. Located 52 km (32.3 mi) from Quito in Pedro Monocayo in Pichincha province, it has an extensive collection of pre-Columbian and pre-Inca Empire ruins. It sits on 84 hectares (210 acres) and is made up of 15 truncated pyramids and 21 tolas (burial mounds) where many skeletons have been found.

Archaeologists believe that Cochasqui was a ceremonial and astronomical center used to calculate the winter and summer solstices to help aid when to plant crops. There is also a legend which has deep roots in Ecuador. The national origin of Ecuador was a result of a union between the conquering Incas and the Ecuadorian Indians who tried to fend them off in Cochasqui.

39. THE INCA'S LASTING IMPRESSION

Once upon a time, the Incas ruled a large part of Western South America. While many associate the Incas with Machu Picchu, Peru's very well-known site, Ecuador has numerous historically relevant sites that are worth a visit.

Rumicucho meaning stone corner in Quechua was built sometime between 1480 and 1500 on a hill 23 km (14.2 mi) north of Quito, a strategic location between two neighboring tribes. It was used by the Incas as a cultivation site because of its fertile land as well as a strategic military point because of its proximity to the equator. The Incas used this site thoroughly until the Spanish conquest in the 1530s.

The Ingapirca ruins in Cañar province are the most significant remnant of the Incans in Ecuador. Inga means Inca and pinca means wall. The walls of these ruins are similar to that of Machu Picchu in that the stone pieces are cut and placed without the use of any adherent. Ingapirca is believed to have been a temple before the Spanish arrived and disassembled big chunks of the wall for their own purposes. Much of the site is still intact and can be visited as a stop along the Pan-American Highway from Quito to Cuenca.

40. THE FESTIVAL OF THE SUN

Inti Raymi (the Festival of the Sun) is one of the most important traditions that came from the Incan empire. From 18-24 June, at the beginning of the summer solstice, many indigenous villages in the Andean highlands of Ecuador honor their most important deity, Inti or the Sun God in Quechua. On this day, a massive party is held to welcome the new agricultural year and give thanks to Pachamama (Mother Nature). During the Incan days, they would pray to Inti using rituals and dances, thanking it for the gift of more daylight to harvest food.

Today, especially in the provinces of Imbabura, Cotopaxi, Tungurahua, Cañar, Azuay, and Loja, the Inti Raymi festival is celebrated with rainbow-colored costumes decorated with mirrors, sequins, and feathers like an Aya Huma (Diablo Huma), a two-faced character. The community selects their Sun Princess, dance to folkloric music, and enjoys delicious food that they harvested from Pachamama.

41. A CHURCH OF GOLD

La Iglesia de la Compañía de Jesús is a Jesuit church located in the historic center of Quito. Inspired by two Roman Jesuit churches, la Compañía as it is known as locally is considered one of the most important works of Spanish Baroque architecture in South America. Its large central nave is covered with gold leaf, gilded plaster, and wood carvings and is covered by green and gold domes. It took over 160 years to construct, but two years after its completion, the Jesuits were forced out of Ecuador and much of the history and architecture of the building were lost. Free guided tours in English and Spanish are offered giving some insight into the church's unique features including perfectly symmetrical elements and syncretism of indigenous faces hidden in the pillars.

42. THE ORCHID CAPITAL IN THE WORLD

Because of Ecuador's diverse climates of dry coastal forests along the Pacific to the damp cloud forests high up the Andes, orchids grow everywhere. The country boasts 4,250 orchid species and 1,301 endemic species, and scientists are discovering more every year since the plants are capable of mutating to adapt to the climate and geography.

The peaceful Jardin Botanico de Quito (Botanic Garden of Quito) in Parque Carolina features an orquideario (orchid greenhouse) of 1,200 species of orchids. The orchids are housed in two massive greenhouses and are watered by three waterfalls. The garden also includes plants from the páramo (high-altitude Andean grasslands), wetlands, and cloud forests. It costs $3.50 to get in and the garden is open every day until late afternoon.

The El Pahuma Orchid Reserve is a privately owned reserve and research center located in a cloud forest in El Pahuma, a one-hour drive from Quito and on the way to Mindo. This small orchid sanctuary has over 300 different species of orchids and is also home to the endangered Spectacled Bear and Plate-billed Mountain Toucan. Visitors can also hike around several trails enjoy the sounds of rushing water and chirping birds. There are rooms available for tourists who want to stay longer and enjoy the beauty around the area.

Jardin Botanico de Guayaquil (Botanic Garden of Guayaquil) has over 700 plant species on display including the Giant Orchid, which can grow up to 2.5 m (8.2 ft) high as well as 75 different species of birds that live in the garden. There is also The Conversation Project Lepidoptario which is trying to preserve endemic butterfly species that have been threatened by the use of pesticides. Entrance is $3 per person.

43. HUMS THE WORD

Ecuador has over 132 species of hummingbirds, which accounts for 40% of the all hummingbird species worldwide. Thanks again to the country's unique geographic makeup, a wide variety of hummingbirds has coexisted within Ecuador's hospitable climates.

The highest concentration of hummingbirds in Ecuador can be found in the cloud forests surrounding Quito known as the Choco-Andes region. The lowlands of the Choco area, which includes Mindo Valley, has the greatest aggregation of restricted-range endemic species including what some consider the most beautiful hummingbird, the Velvet Purple Coronet.

The high-altitude region of Yanacocha located near Pichincha Volcano is another great place to go hummingbird watching. This area is home to the critically endangered Black-breasted Puffleg, the symbolic bird of Quito.

The Tumbesian lowlands along the coast are another great area to look for hummingbirds because of its high concentration of restricted-range birds and great diversity of vegetation.

44. OLINGUITOS

The olinguito is the first carnivorous mammal to be discovered in the Western Hemisphere in the 21st century. Known colloquially as "kitty bear" because of its large eyes and wooly red or orange-brown fur, it was discovered in 2013 living in the cloud forests in western Ecuador, thus giving the species name of neblina (fog or mist).

Even though the olinguito is new to the science world, people have been living in or near its habitat for centuries. Specimens of olinguitos have been sitting in museums for many years, and one live olinguito called several zoos in the US home during the 1960s and 1970s because these animals were misidentified.

Olinguitos are quite hard to spot in the wild as they are nocturnal and love jumping from tree to tree in the forest canopies. However, there has been a report of an olinguito who regularly visits the Bellavista cloud forest in Tandayapa near Quito.

45. BIODIVERSITY IN ONE PARK

Yasuní National Park, located in the eastern part of the country on the Ecuadorian-Peruvian border, is within the confines of the Amazon Rainforest. The park is considered the most biologically diverse places in the world even though it covers 0.15% of the Amazon Basin. There are over 150 different amphibian species in the park, which is more than the United States and Canada combined. There are 121 documented species of reptiles and 382 known species of fish. At least 596 different species of birds live in Yasuní, which makes up one-third of the total native species in the Amazon. There are also 117 particular species of bats and over 100,000 species of insects, which is the same amount as that of the North American continent.

Yasuní is also home to some of the last remaining indigenous people from the Amazon. The Tagaeri and Taromenane tribes continue to live independently in the rainforest and have fought to keep the outside world from invading and destroying their ancient culture. In 1999, the southern part of the park as an "untouchable zone" to help secure the rights of these people.

A four-day tour to Yasuní starts at $1,000. A cheaper option to explore the park is to situate yourself in the town of Tena and do day trips into the jungle.

46. THE DANCE OF THE DEVIL

From 1-6 January every year, a bizarre celebration is held in Píllaro, a town in Tungurahua province. In La Diablada de Píllaro, thousands of imps parade on the streets to the dance of the Diablada. This celebration originates from the colonial era when the indigenous people and the Mestizo (Spanish and native descents) joined together to rebel against the Catholic religion. Three main characters take part in this party: devils, guarichas (women who are pregnant out of wedlock), and capariches (floor sweepers). These figures represent people's refusal to accept the church as well as the physical economic, psychological, and moral abuse they suffered because of the Spanish. This ritual was done in the new year, which coincides with the Holy Innocents Feast, to achieve better levels of mental health and resistance. By disguising themselves as they when they fear the most, they gain control over evil powers.

Nowadays, the festival goes beyond local communities. People for all over Ecuador, including the older population, women, children, and foreigners take part in the celebration. Preparation for this festival takes place months in advance as the dancers practice to coordinate their movements along with musicians and ringleaders of the parade. It is believed that if you dress as the devil in this festival, you must do so seven consecutive times to prevent strange things from happening to you.

47. HANGING OUT WITH GIANTS

During the days of colonialization, to combat yellow fever left behind by the Spanish, many locals burned their clothes. The citizens of Guayaquil took this burning notion even further by adding masks to their infected wardrobes creating effigies, demonizing the perceived "enemies of the people". Over time, this ritual evolved. In the Astillero shipyard neighborhood, children collect wood chips and sawdust to fill massive papier maché puppets to burn on the last day of the year.

For two weeks before the year finishes, on La Ruta de los Gigantes (The Road of the Giants), massive characters towering 9 m (29.5 ft) high from fiction, fantasy, politics, and sports line Avenida 6 de Marzo. Local artists spend months creating these masterpieces that will be set on fire. Right before midnight on 31 December, under the watchful eye of firefighters, these giants are burned marking the end of that year's chapter and beginning next year with new promises and challenges.

48. THE TELEFERIQO

The TeleferiQo in Quito is one of the best ways to see the capital from high above. This gondola lift starts on the east side of Pichincha Volcano at 3,117 m (10,226 ft) and finishes at 3,945 m (12,943 ft) traveling 2,237 linear meters in roughly twenty minutes to the Cruz Loma viewpoint making this one of the highest aerial trams in the world. After exiting the TeleferiQo, you can hike up to the summit of Rucu Pichincha for a higher view of the city. The trek takes about five hours round trip, but there are plenty of places to relax afterward before taking the ride back down. Just be aware that the weather on top varies dramatically from the base of the lift, but generally, the top is cold and windy. The weather is better in the mornings, especially on a clear day when the views are amazing. It costs $8.50 for foreigners for a round trip.

The visitor center at the base includes the VulQano Park, an amusement park, several restaurants, and a food court, the world's highest go-kart track, and other attractions.

49. THE UGLIER SIDE OF QUITO

The abandoned Garcia Moreno prison is located in the San Roque neighborhood in the south of Quito. The former president of Ecuador, General Eloy Alfaro, lived in this prison until his untimely death. Corrupt politicians, con men, a teenage serial killer, and a notorious Colombian murderer also called Garcia Moreno home. The prison was left as is when it shut down in 2014 due to overcrowding. Old clothes, outdated magazines, images of Jesus Christ and the Virgin Mary, and uplifting messages written on the walls remain in this converted museum. The 2-hour day and night tours are given by former prison guards, which offers an insightful look into life inside a prison.

50. THE TOPIARY GARDEN OF TULCÁN

For an off-the-beaten-track location, look no further than Tulcán, the capital of Carchi province. This small city on the border of Ecuador and Colombia has a cemetery with elaborately-trimmed cypress bushes. Founded in 1932, the town's cemetery was built to replace the one severely damaged by an earthquake in 1923. The soil in the new plot was favorable for the growth of cypress trees. The head of the park ordered rows of cypresses to be planted on the premises. He then started pruning each tree to various pre-Colombian, Augustinian, and Arabic totems. Other trees were shaped into mythological characters, animals, or simple geometric shapes. In total, over 300 trees were modeled into works of art. Today, the legacy of the topiary garden now is maintained by the park head's five sons.

TOP REASONS TO BOOK THIS TRIP

Nature: Where else can you find such biodiversity in one country?

Volcanoes: From this highest peak in the world to some of the world's most active volcanoes, Ecuador has plenty to see.

Tradition: Ecuador is a multicultural nation with one of the largest indigenous populations in South America. The country is constantly changing while maintaining the deep traditions of the past.

OTHER RESOURCES:

https://ecuador.travel/

http://www.ecuador.com/tourism/

https://www.lonelyplanet.com/ecuador

https://wikitravel.org/en/Ecuador

BONUS BOOK

50 THINGS TO KNOW ABOUT PACKING LIGHT FOR TRAVEL

PACK THE RIGHT WAY EVERY TIME

AUTHOR: MANIDIPA BHATTACHARYYA

Edited by Melanie Howthorne

ABOUT THE AUTHOR

Manidipa Bhattacharyya is a creative writer and editor, with an
education in English literature and Linguistics. After working in the IT
industry for seven long years she decided to call it quits and follow her
heart instead. Manidipa has been ghost writing, editing, proof reading
and doing secondary research services for many story tellers and article
writers for about three years. She stays in Kolkata, India with her
husband and a busy two year old. In her own time Manidipa enjoys
travelling, photography and writing flash fiction.

Manidipa believes in travelling light and never carries anything that she
couldn't haul herself on a trip. However, travelling with her child
changed the scenario. She seemed to carry the entire world with her for
the baby on the first two trips. But good sense prevailed and she is
again working her way to becoming a light traveler, this time with a
kid.

INTRODUCTION

He who would travel happily
must travel light.

-Antoine de Saint-Exupéry

Travel takes you to different places from seas and mountains to deserts and much more. In your travels you get to interact with different people and their cultures. You will, however, enjoy the sights and interact positively with these new people even more, if you are travelling light.

When you travel light your mind can be free from worry about your belongings. You do not have to spend precious vacation time waiting for your luggage to arrive after a long flight. There is be no chance of your bags going missing and the best part is that you need not pay a fee for checked baggage.

People who have mastered this art of packing light will root for you to take only one carry-on, wherever you go. However, many people can find it really hard to pack light. More so if you are travelling with children. Differentiating between "must have" and "just in case" items is the starting point. There will be ample shopping avenues at your destination which are just waiting to be explored.

This book will show you 'packing' in a new 'light' – pun intended – and help you to embrace light packing practices for all of your future travels.

Off to packing!

DEDICATION

I dedicate this book to all the travel buffs that I know, who have given me great insights into the contents of their backpacks.

THE RIGHT TRAVEL GEAR

1. CHOOSE YOUR TRAVEL GEAR CAREFULLY

While selecting your travel gear, pick items that are light weight, durable and most importantly, easy to carry. There are cases with wheels so you can drag them along – these are usually on the heavy side because of the trolley. Alternatively a backpack that you can carry comfortably on your back, or even a duffel bag that you can carry easily by hand or sling across your body are also great options. Whatever you choose, one thing to keep in mind is that the luggage itself should not weigh a ton, this will give you the flexibility to bring along one extra pair of shoes if you so desire.

2. CARRY THE MINIMUM NUMBER OF BAGS

Selecting light weight luggage is not everything. You need to restrict the number of bags you carry as well. One carry-on size bag is ideal for light travel. Most carriers allow one cabin baggage plus one purse, handbag or camera bag as long as it slides under the seat in front. So technically, you can carry two items of luggage without checking them in.

3. PACK ONE EXTRA BAG

Always pack one extra empty bag along with your essential items. This could be a very light weight duffel bag or even a sturdy tote bag which takes up minimal space. In the event that you end up buying a lot of souvenirs, you already have a handy bag to stuff all that into and do not have to spend time hunting for an appropriate bag.

I'm very strict with my packing and have everything in its right place. I never change a rule. I hardly use anything in the hotel room. I wheel my own wardrobe in and that's it.

Charlie Watts

CLOTHES & ACCESSORIES

4. PLAN AHEAD

Figure out in advance what you plan to do on your trip. That will help you to pick that one dress you need for the occasion. If you are going to attend a wedding then you have to carry formal wear. If not, you can ditch the gown for something lighter that will be comfortable during long walks or on the beach.

5. WEAR THAT JACKET

Remember that wearing items will not add extra luggage for your air travel. So wear that bulky jacket that you plan to carry for your trip. This saves space and can also help keep you warm during the chilly flight.

6. MIX AND MATCH

Carry clothes that can be interchangeably used to reinvent your look. Find one top that goes well with a couple of pairs of pants or skirts. Use tops, shirts and jackets wisely along with other accessories like a scarf or a stole to create a new look.

7. CHOOSE YOUR FABRIC WISELY

Stuffing clothes in cramped bags definitely takes its toll which results in wrinkles. It is best to carry wrinkle free, synthetic clothes or merino tops. This will eliminate the need for that small iron you usually bring along.

8. DITCH CLOTHES PACK UNDERWEAR

Pack more underwear and socks. These are the things that will give you a fresh feel even if you do not get a chance to wear fresh clothes. Moreover these are easy to wash and can be dried inside the hotel room itself.

9. CHOOSE DARK OVER LIGHT

While picking your clothes choose dark coloured ones. They are easy to colour coordinate and can last longer before needing a wash. Accidental food spills and dirt from the road are less visible on darker clothes.

10. WEAR YOUR JEANS

Take only one pair of Jeans with you, which you should wear on the flight. Remember to pick a pair that can be worn for sightseeing trips and is equally eloquent for dinner. You can add variety by adding light weight cargoes and chinos.

11. CARRY SMART ACCESSORIES

The right accessory can give you a fresh look even with the same old dress. An intelligent neck-piece, a couple of bright scarves, stoles or a sarong can be used in a number of ways to add variety to your clothing. These light weight beauties can double up as a nursing cover, a light blanket, beach wear, a modesty cover for visiting places of worship, and also makes for an enthralling game of peek-a-boo.

12. LEARN TO FOLD YOUR GARMENTS

Seasoned travellers all swear by rolling their clothes for compact and wrinkle free packing. Bundle packing, where you roll the clothes around a central object as if tying it up, is also a popular method of compact and wrinkle free packing. Stacking folded clothes one on top of another is a big no-no as it makes creases extreme and they are difficult to get rid of without ironing.

13. WASH YOUR DIRTY LAUNDRY

One of the ways to avoid carrying loads of clothes is to wash the clothes you carry. At some places you might get to use the laundry services or a Laundromat but if you are in a pinch, best solution is to wash them yourself. If that is the plan then carrying quick drying clothes is highly recommended, which most often also happen to be the wrinkle free variety.

14. LEAVE THOSE TOWELS BEHIND

Regular towels take up a lot of space, are heavy and take ages to dry out. If you are staying at hotels they will provide you with towels anyway. If you are travelling to a remote place, where the availability of towels look doubtful, carry a light weight travel towel of viscose material to do the job.

15. USE A COMPRESSION BAG

Compression bags are getting lots of recommendation now days from regular travellers. These are useful for saving space in your luggage when you have to pack bulky dresses. While packing for the return trip, get help from the hotel staff to arrange a vacuum cleaner.

FOOTWEAR

16. PUT ON YOUR HIKING BOOTS

If you have plans to go hiking or trekking during your trip, you will need those bulky hiking boots. The best way to carry them is to wear them on flight to save space and luggage weight. You can remove the boots once inside and be comfortable in your socks.

17. PICKING THE RIGHT SHOES

Shoes are often the bulkiest items, along with being the dainty if you are a female. They need care and take up a lot of space in your luggage. It is advisable therefore to pick shoes very carefully. If you plan to do a lot of walking and site seeing, then wearing a pair of comfortable walking shoes are a must. For more formal occasions you can carry durable, light weight flats which will not take up much space.

18. STUFF SHOES

If you happen to pack a pair of shoes, ensure you utilize their hollow insides. Tuck small items like rolled up socks or belts to save space. They will also be easy to find.

TOILETRIES

19. STASHING TOILETRIES

Carry only absolute necessities. Airline rules dictate that for one carry-on bag, liquids and gels must be in 3.4 ounce (100ml) bottles or less, and must be packed in a one quart zip-lock bag. If you are planning to stay in a hotel, the basic things will be provided for you. It's best is to buy the rest from the local market at your destination.

20. TAKE ALONG TAMPONS

Tampons are a hard to find item in a lot of countries. Figure out how many you need and pack accordingly. For longer stays you can buy them online and have them delivered to where you are staying.

21. GET PAMPERED BEFORE YOU TRAVEL

Some avid travellers suggest getting a pedicure and manicure just the day before travelling. This not only gives you a well kept look, you also save the trouble of packing nail polish. Remember, every little bit of weight reduced adds up.

ELECTRONICS

22. LUGGING ALONG ELECTRONICS

Electronics have a large role to play in our lives today. Most of us cannot imagine our lives away from our phones, laptops or tablets. However while travelling, one must consider the amount of weight these electronics add to our luggage. Thankfully smart phones come along with all the essentials tools like a camera, email access, picture editing tools and more. They are smart to the point of eliminating the need to carry multiple gadgets. Choose a smart phone that suits all your requirements and travel with the world in your palms or pocket.

23. REDUCE THE NUMBER OF CHARGERS

If you do travel with multiple electronic devices, you will have to bear the additional burden of carrying all their chargers too. Check if a single charger can be used for multiple devices. You might also consider investing in a pocket charger. These small devices support multiple devices while keeping you charged on the go.

24. TRAVEL FRIENDLY APPS

Along with smart phones come numerous apps, which are immensely helpful in our travels. You name it and you have an app for it at hand – take pictures, sharing with friends and family, torch to light dark roads, maps, checking flight/train times, find hotels and many other things. Use these smart alternatives to traditional items like books to eliminate weight and save space.

I get ideas about what's essential when packing my suitcase.

-Diane von Furstenberg

TRAVELLING WITH KIDS

25. BRING ALONG THE STROLLER

Kids might enjoy walking for a while but they soon tire out and a stroller is the just the right thing for them to rest in while you continue your tour. Strollers also double duty as a luggage carrier and shopping bag holder. Remember to pick a light weight, easy to handle brand of stroller. Better yet, find out in advance if you can rent a stroller at your destination.

26. BRING ONLY ENOUGH DIAPERS FOR YOUR TRIP

Diapers take up a lot of space and add to the weight of your luggage. Therefore it is advisable to carry just enough diapers to last through the trip and a few for afterwards, till you buy fresh stock at your destination. Unless of course you are travelling to a really remote area, in which case you have no choice but to carry the load. Otherwise diapers are something you will find pretty easily.

27. TAKE ONLY A COUPLE OF TOYS

Children are easily attracted by new things in their environment. While travelling they will find numerous 'new' objects to scrutinize and play with. Packing just one favorite toy is enough, or if there is no favorite toy leave out all of them in favor of stories or imaginary games.

28. CARRY KID FRIENDLY SNACKS

Create a small snack counter in your bag to store away quick bites for those sudden hunger pangs. Depending on the child's age this could include chocolates, raisins, dry fruits, granola bars or biscuits. Also keep a bottle of water handy for your little one.

These things do not add much weight and can be adjusted in a handbag or knapsack.

29. GAMES TO CARRY

Create some travel specific, imaginary games if you have slightly grown up children, like spot the attractions. Keep a coloring book and colors handy for in-flight or hotel time. Apps on your smart phone can keep the children engaged with cartoons and story books. Older children are often entertained by games available on phones or tablets. This cuts the weight of luggage down while keeping the kids entertained.

30. LET THE KIDS CARRY THEIR LOAD

A good thing is to start early sharing of responsibilities. Let your child pick a bag of his or her choice and pack it themselves. Keep tabs on what they are stuffing in their bags by asking if they will be using that item on the trip. It could start out being just an entertainment bag initially but with growing years they will learn to sort the useful from the superfluous. Children as little as four can maneuver a small trolley suitcase like a pro- their experience in pull along toys credit. If you are worried that you may be pulling it for them, you may want to start with a backpack.

31. DECIDE ON LOCATION FOR CHILDREN TO SLEEP

While on a trip you might not always get a crib at your destination, and carrying one will make life all the more difficult. Instead call ahead to see if there are any cribs or roll out beds for children. You may even put blankets on the floor. Weave them a story about camping and they will gladly sleep without any trouble.

32. GET BABY PRODUCTS DELIVERED AT YOUR DESTINATION

If you are absolutely paranoid about not getting your favourite variety of diaper or brand of baby food, check out online stores like amazon.com for services in your destination city. You can buy things online ahead of your travel and get them delivered to your hotel upon arrival.

33. FEEDING NEEDS OF YOUR INFANTS

If you are travelling with a breastfed infant, you save the trouble of carrying bottles and bottle sanitization kits. For special food, or medications, you may need

to call ahead to make sure you have a refrigerator
where you are staying.

34. FEEDING NEEDS OF YOUR TODDLER

With the progression from infancy to toddler, their
dietary requirements too evolve. You will have to
pack some snacks for travelling time. Fresh fruits and
vegetables can be purchased at your destination. Most
of the cities you travel to in whichever part of the
world, will have baby food products and formulas,
available at the local drug-store or the supermarket.

35. PICKING CLOTHES FOR YOUR BABY

Contrary to popular belief, babies can do without
many changes of clothes. At the most pack 2 outfits
per day. Pack mix and match type clothes for your
little one as well. Pick things which are comfortable
to wear and quick to dry.

36. SELECTING SHOES FOR YOUR BABY

Like outfits, kids can make do with two pairs of
comfortable shoes. If you can get some water
resistant shoes it will be best. To expedite drying wet
shoes, you can stuff newspaper in them then wrap

them with newspaper and leave them to dry overnight.

37. KEEP ONE CHANGE OF CLOTHES HANDY

Travelling with kids can be tricky. Keep a change of clothes for the kids and mum handy in your purse or tote bag. This takes a bit of space in your hand luggage but comes extremely handy in case there are any accidents or spills.

38. LEAVE BEHIND BABY ACCESSORIES

Baby accessories like their bed, bath tub, car seat, crib etc. should be left at home. Many hotels provide a crib on request, while car seats can be borrowed from friends or rented. Babies can be given a bath in the hotel sink or even in the adult bath tub with a little bit of water. If you bring a few bath toys, they can be used in the bath, pool, and out of water. They can also be sanitized easily in the sink.

39. CARRY A SMALL LOAD OF PLASTIC BAGS

With children around there are chances of a number of soiled clothes and diapers. These plastic bags help to sort the dirt from the clean inside your big bag.

These are very light weight and come in handy to other carry stuff as well at times.

PACK WITH A PURPOSE

40. PACKING FOR BUSINESS TRIPS

One neutral-colored suit should suffice. It can be paired with different shirts, ties and accessories for different occasions. One pair of black suit pants could be worn with a matching jacket for the office or with a snazzy top for dinner.

41. PACKING FOR A CRUISE

Most cruises have formal dinners, and that formal dress usually takes up a lot of space. However you might find a tuxedo to rent. For women, a short black dress with multiple accessory options will do the trick.

42. PACKING FOR A LONG TRIP OVER DIFFERENT CLIMATES

The secret packing mantra for travel over multiple climates is layering. Layering traps air around your body creating insulation against the cold. The same light t-shirt that is comfortable in a warmer climate can be the innermost layer in a colder climate.

REDUCE SOME MORE WEIGHT

43. LEAVE PRECIOUS THINGS AT HOME

Things that you would hate to lose or get damaged leave them at home. Precious jewelry, expensive gadgets or dresses, could be anything. You will not require these on your trip. Leave them at home and spare the load on your mind.

44. SEND SOUVENIRS BY MAIL

If you have spent all your money on purchasing souvenirs, carrying them back in the same bag that you brought along would be difficult. Either pack everything in another bag and check it in the airport or get everything shipped to your home. Use an international carrier for a secure transit, but this could be more expensive than the checking fees at the airport.

45. AVOID CARRYING BOOKS

Books equal to weight. There are many reading apps which you can download on your smart phone or tab.

Plus there are gadgets like Kindle and Nook that are thinner and lighter alternatives to your regular book.

CHECK, GET, SET, CHECK AGAIN

46. STRATEGIZE BEFORE PACKING

Create a travel list and prepare all that you think you need to carry along. Keep everything on your bed or floor before packing and then think through once again – do I really need that? Any item that meets this question can be avoided. Remove whatever you don't really need and pack the rest.

47. TEST YOUR LUGGAGE

Once you have fully packed for the trip take a test trip with your luggage. Take your bags and go to town for window shopping for an hour. If you enjoy your hour long trip it is good to go, if not, go home and reduce the load some more. Repeat this test till you hit the right weight.

48. ADD A ROLL OF DUCT TAPE

You might wonder why, when this book has been talking about reducing stuff, we're suddenly asking you to pack something totally unusual. This is because when you have limited supplies, duct tape is immensely helpful for small repairs – a broken bag, leaking zip-lock bag, broken sunglasses, you name it and duct tape can fix it, temporarily.

49. LIST OF ESSENTIAL ITEMS

Even though the emphasis is on packing light, there are things which have to be carried for any trip. Here is our list of essentials:

•Passport/Visa or any other ID

•Any other paper work that might be required on a trip like permits, hotel reservation confirmations etc.

•Medicines – all your prescription medicines and emergency kit, especially if you are travelling with children

•Medical or vaccination records

•Money in foreign currency if travelling to a different country

•Tickets- Email or Message them to your phone

50. MAKE THE MOST OF YOUR TRIP

Wherever you are going, whatever you hope to do we encourage you to embrace it whole-heartedly. Take in the scenery, the culture and above all, enjoy your time away from home.

On a long journey even a straw weighs heavy.

-Spanish Proverb

PACKING AND PLANNING TIPS

A Week before Leaving

- Arrange for someone to take care of pets and water plants.

- Stop mail and newspaper.

- Notify Credit Card companies where you are going.

- Change your thermostat settings.

- Car inspected, oil is changed, and tires have the correct pressure.

- Passports and photo identification is up to date.

- Pay bills.

- Copy important items and download travel Apps.

- Start collecting small bills for tips.

Right Before Leaving

- Clean out refrigerator.

- Empty garbage cans.

- Lock windows.

- Make sure you have the proper identification with you.

- Bring cash for tips.

- Remember travel documents.

- Lock door behind you.

- Remember wallet.

- Unplug items in house and pack chargers.

READ OTHER
GREATER THAN A TOURIST
BOOKS

Greater Than a Tourist San Miguel de Allende Guanajuato Mexico:
50 Travel Tips from a Local by Tom Peterson

Greater Than a Tourist – Lake George Area New York USA:
50 Travel Tips from a Local by Janine Hirschklau

Greater Than a Tourist – Monterey California United States:
50 Travel Tips from a Local by Katie Begley

Greater Than a Tourist – Chanai Crete Greece:
50 Travel Tips from a Local by Dimitra Papagrigoraki

Greater Than a Tourist – The Garden Route Western Cape Province
South Africa: 50 Travel Tips from a Local by Li-Anne McGregor van
Aardt

Greater Than a Tourist – Sevilla Andalusia Spain:
50 Travel Tips from a Local by Gabi Gazon

Greater Than a Tourist – Kota Bharu Kelantan Malaysia:
50 Travel Tips from a Local by Aditi Shukla

Children's Book: Charlie the Cavalier Travels the World by Lisa
Rusczyk

> TOURIST

Visit Greater Than a Tourist for Free Travel Tips
http://GreaterThanATourist.com

Sign up for the Greater Than a Tourist Newsletter for
discount days, new books, and travel information:
http://eepurl.com/cxspyf

Follow us on Facebook for tips, images, and ideas:
https://www.facebook.com/GreaterThanATourist

Follow us on Pinterest for travel tips and ideas:
http://pinterest.com/GreaterThanATourist

Follow us on Instagram for beautiful travel images:
http://Instagram.com/GreaterThanATourist

>TOURIST

> TOURIST

Please leave your honest review of this book on Amazon and Goodreads. Please send your feedback to GreaterThanaTourist@gmail.com as we continue to improve the series. We appreciate your positive and constructive feedback. Thank you.

METRIC CONVERSIONS

TEMPERATURE

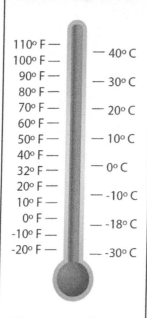

110° F — — 40° C
100° F —
90° F — — 30° C
80° F —
70° F — — 20° C
60° F —
50° F — — 10° C
40° F —
32° F — — 0° C
20° F —
10° F — — -10° C
0° F —
-10° F — — -18° C
-20° F — — -30° C

To convert F to C:

Subtract 32, and then multiply by 5/9 or .5555.

To Convert C to F:

Multiply by 1.8 and then add 32.

32F = 0C

LIQUID VOLUME

To Convert:.................Multiply by
U.S. Gallons to Liters................. 3.8
U.S. Liters to Gallons 26
Imperial Gallons to U.S. Gallons 1.2
Imperial Gallons to Liters....... 4.55
Liters to Imperial Gallons 22
1 Liter = .26 U.S. Gallon
1 U.S. Gallon = 3.8 Liters

DISTANCE

To convert ....Multiply by
Inches to Centimeters 2.54
Centimeters to Inches 39
Feet to Meters....................... .3
Meters to Feet 3.28
Yards to Meters 91
Meters to Yards 1.09
Miles to Kilometers 1.61
Kilometers to Miles............ .62
1 Mile = 1.6 km
1 km = .62 Miles

WEIGHT

1 Ounce = .28 Grams
1 Pound = .4555 Kilograms
1 Gram = .04 Ounce
1 Kilogram = 2.2 Pounds

TRAVEL QUESTIONS

- Do you bring presents home to family or friends after a vacation?

- Do you get motion sick?

- Do you have a favorite billboard?

- Do you know what to do if there is a flat tire?

- Do you like a sun roof open?

- Do you like to eat in the car?

- Do you like to wear sun glasses in the car?

- Do you like toppings on your ice cream?

- Do you use public bathrooms?

- Did you bring your cell phone and does it have power?

- Do you have a form of identification with you?

- Have you ever been pulled over by a cop?

- Have you ever given money to a stranger on a road trip?

- Have you ever taken a road trip with animals?

- Have you ever went on a vacation alone?

- Have you ever run out of gas?

- If you could move to any place in the world, where would it be?

- If you could travel anywhere in the world, where would you travel?

- If you could travel in any vehicle, which one would it be?

- If you had three things to wish for from a magic genie, what would they be?

- If you have a driver's license, how many times did it take you to pass the test?

- What are you the most afraid of on vacation?

- What do you want to get away from the most when you are on vacation?

- What foods smells bad to you?

- What item do you bring on ever trip with you away from home?

- What makes you sleepy?

- What song would you love to hear on the radio when you're cruising on the highway?

- What travel job would you want the least?

- What will you miss most while you are away from home?

- What is something you always wanted to try?

- What is the best road side attraction that you ever saw?

- What is the farthest distance you ever biked?

- What is the farthest distance you ever walked?

- What is the weirdest thing you needed to buy while on vacation?

- What is your favorite candy?

- What is your favorite color car?

- What is your favorite family vacation?

- What is your favorite food?

- What is your favorite gas station drink or food?

- What is your favorite license plate design?

- What is your favorite restaurant?

- What is your favorite smell?

- What is your favorite song?

- What is your favorite sound that nature makes?

- What is your favorite thing to bring home from a vacation?

- What is your favorite vacation with friends?

- What is your favorite way to relax?

- Where is the farthest place you ever traveled in a car?

- Where is the farthest place you ever went North, South, East and West?

- Where is your favorite place in the world?

- Who is your favorite singer?

- Who taught you how to drive?

- Who will you miss the most while you are away?

- Who if the first person you will contact when you get to your destination?

- Who brought you on your first vacation?

- Who likes to travel the most in your life?

- Would you rather be hot or cold?

- Would you rather drive above, below, or at the speed limited?

- Would you rather drive on a highway or a back road?

- Would you rather go on a train or a boat?

- Would you rather go to the beach or the woods?

TRAVEL BUCKET LIST

1.

2.

3.

4.

5.

6.

7.

8.

9.

10.

NOTES

Made in United States
Orlando, FL
11 March 2024

44656036R00082